Beyond Bitcoin

How to Reinvent

the World with

Your Own Currency

ADAM SAVAGE

Copyright © 2017 Adam Savage

All rights reserved.

ISBN-13:
978-1979804103
ISBN-10:
1979804109

Money is the blood of civilization. It controls where people are, what they do, and how they behave. People obsess over it, worry about it, study it, and worship it. For better or worse, it is the largest indicator of "success" in the modern world. Yet for all the attention we give it, rarely do we think about what it really *is*.

The key thing to remember about money is this: *We created it.* Without people, there is no money. A basic understanding of math is necessary to use it. Other animals may trade things, but only humans have bank accounts, credit cards, mortgages, student loans, retirement accounts, lease programs, insurance, stocks, bonds, and many more ways of manipulating money.

Initially, money took various forms. Shiny rocks, blood on animal fur, notches in wood – these and other methods were used to signify *debt*. If I was a farmer 4000 years ago and I couldn't grow enough crop to feed my family, I might ask a nearby farmer for help. He could give me some of his crop. In exchange, I could give him five pieces of silver I had found. This would tell him that I had borrowed five bushels of wheat, and that I would return them to him in the next harvest. The silver itself was worthless – it had no practical use.

Once I had his food, I could ignore the debt and never repay him. But the debt was based on trust. If I didn't pay him back, it would weaken my standing in the community. Perhaps my neighbor would badmouth me to others. *He* certainly wouldn't ever give me food again.

Money's strength is that it allows people to interact. As societies grew to encompass empires of thousands, money allowed *total strangers* to interact. This is essentially what civilization is: Domesticated primates living in close proximity and trusting one another. There are degrees of trust, obviously, but for the most part, people learn to put enormous trust in total strangers. When you eat a sandwich in a restaurant, you trust that it won't be poisoned. When you fly in an airplane, you trust that the pilot will get you safely to your destination. When you turn on the faucet, you trust that somebody somewhere has provided you with generally safe water. Implicit trust is everywhere in countless social contracts.

Sometimes these contracts are violated. When a small social contract is violated, we say that someone is "rude." When a large social contract is violated, we call it a "crime."

For the most part, society works. There are periodic breakdowns, but it is generally reliable. It would be impossible to have a global society if you had to know everyone you interacted with. This is the strength of national or international currencies: I can spend my money anywhere my money is used, regardless of who I am.

But there are also great weaknesses to money, in its present form. One problem is that some people and companies are *very* good at accumulating it. Apple Inc., for instance, has total assets in excess of $300 billion. Warren Buffett, as of 2017, has a net worth of about $76 billion. While it's wonderful for them and shows the power of capitalism, it extracts value from the rest of the economy. Instead of creating interaction, this money is held and invested in complicated investment vehicles. It creates more wealth for those who possess it, but they quickly arrive at a point where their income exceeds their ability to spend it.

Another huge issue with the current economy is our reliance on *debt*. It is found throughout modern societies. Both individually and at the government level, debt, credit, mortgages (different names for the same basic concept) slow a culture down and constrict prosperity. They create the illusion of flexibility, which they offer in the short term, at the expense of long-term stagnation. People take on dead-end jobs and economies are riddled by taxes to make interest payments to foreign investors.

The US National Debt is approaching $20 trillion. Every year *billions* are spent by taxpayers simply to pay the *interest* on this debt. The amount varies each year, but the interest is typically between $400 and $500 billion dollars each year. Think of all the healthcare and education this money could buy if our budget wasn't so crippled by debt.

In addition, most individuals in the U.S. carry some form of personal debt. This takes many forms: credit card debt, student loan debt, car payments, mortgages, and more. These are constraints at the individual level, and they prevent people from reaching their full potential.

Even without debt, there is great dissatisfaction with how tax dollars are spent. The United States, for instance, is an enormous country with a representative government. A republic like this made sense when the country was founded. People in cities were the minority. Most people lived in rural environments, and farming was a major source of employment. Communication across the country could take weeks. It made sense to send a representative hundreds or thousands of miles to Washington DC. A representative might not be completely in line with how you'd vote, but it allowed a community to have representation at the national level.

We live in a very different world now. Agricultural workers are increasingly being replaced by machines, and most people live in cities. In addition, communication is instantaneous. People take an increased interest in governing themselves and in directly choosing where their tax dollars go. The partisan divide has also grown more extreme thanks to online funnels. The internet makes it easy to mentally surround yourself with opinions you agree with.

If you do disagree with how your tax dollars are used, what are your options? Obviously you can refuse to pay your income tax. But this is a crime that you may quickly regret. Besides, it is very difficult to avoid all forms of taxation. Many state and local governments charge sales tax. Whether you see it or not, taxes are extracted from your income.

What other options do you have then? Cryptocurrencies are one answer. Based on the blockchain technology, cryptocurrencies allow the creation of digital money. The popularity of this money has skyrocketed in recent years. If you had $1,000 in Bitcoin currency in 2010, it would be worth millions in 2017. A huge number of speculators started buying Bitcoin several years ago, unnaturally inflating its value. This kind of growth is not sustainable, however, and many people talk about a Bitcoin "bubble." This refers to a commodity that has been overvalued. Bitcoin will most likely lose significant value at some point. But a bubble draws attention to Bitcoin's growing popularity. It and other cryptocurrencies have advantages over other national currencies. For instance, they may be used internationally, are less regulated and taxed, and may be difficult to track. This has led to their use by criminals to purchases drugs and firearms, but there are also legitimate uses to these currencies.

Despite the possibilities for cryptocurrencies, most of them have a similar weakness to standard currency: Their value is rather arbitrary, and the currency does little for the society itself.. Bitcoin may be derived by "mining" the coin using computations that have a value, ensuring the blockchain is accurate for accounting, but it is largely useless to the community at large.

The point is that money, in its current structure – whether currency that is arbitrarily printed by the government or cryptocurrency with value assigned by machines – does little to benefit us. It lets us interact less and less. The good news is that we can start thinking about money in new ways. Because we created money, we can also reinvent it and *design* it to guarantee our benefit.

My own background is in education, and I think education is key to a society's success or failure. As Nelson Mandela put it, "Education is the great engine of personal development. It is through education that the daughter of a peasant can become a doctor, that the son of a mineworker can become the head of the mine, that a child of farm workers can become the president of a great nation. It is what we make out of what we have, not what we are given, that separates one person from another."

Education creates opportunities for people by allowing new career paths to open. Education reduces the crime rate. This is especially significant in the United States, which has the highest incarceration rate in the world. The average cost to keep a prisoner per year in the United States is $31,286! It makes sense to do what we can to keep people out of prison. This is one more example of an inefficient use of money.

Despite its benefits, traditional education is very expensive in the U.S. The average class of 2016 college graduate left school with $37,172 in student loan debt.

Meanwhile, Donald Trump claims to be adding jobs to the U.S. economy in sectors like coal mining.

But coal mining, like many industries, is losing jobs to automation. Like factory and construction jobs, robots and other machines are replacing human workers. Trying to force humans to do jobs that machines can do better is pointless. Besides, jobs like coal mining *should* be handled by machines. It is monotonous and often leads to health problems like black lung disease. Better to move workers into industries in high demand: Programming, Engineering, Data Science, Robotics, Medicine, and Energy Science, for instance.

It would be great if a coal miner could immediately transition into a new career, but that's not realistic. Many of them have families to support. Even if coal miners want to learn new skills, they lack the time and money to allow it. But the fact remains that education can solve many of our problems.

The solution, as I see it, is to connect money with education in a completely new way. Instead of charging people to go to school, we must lower the cost so there is no fee to attend. Free school is great, but we can take it one step further: *We can pay people to attend school.* The goal of education-based currencies is to allow people time and money to pursue education, which will benefit society more than manual labor.

Before we get into the details of how we make this possible, the benefits to this scenario are immediately apparent. Anyone with the desire to go to school would be able to. Anyone lacking a skill could now afford to fill the holes in their knowledge. Anyone who can't find a job can enter school-based internship programs to gain experience. Anyone knee-deep in debt doesn't have to let it keep them from going to school. Anyone considering theft, selling drugs or other contraband, or other illegal activities to support themselves, will no longer have that as an excuse.

And when I say *anyone*, I mean anyone. For this system to work, we must allow people of any age or background to participate. Education can be a right guaranteed to you as a human, pure and simple. I think we will look back on the time when education was based on position and money as extremely unjust – and more significantly, counterproductive to the health of the society.

This may sound similar to *Universal Basic Income*, a term that has recently grown in popularity. It supplants previous ideas about socialism and the welfare state. Experiments are already taking place in certain governments and at the local level to see if they help a society as a whole. While conservatives might balk at the idea of handing out money for nothing, the results cannot be ignored. It may well produce less strain on society. Reducing prison inmates and emergency room visits (due to lack of medical insurance) are two notable ways that universal basic income can strengthen an economy. But for those who are worried that people will sponge off others and not contribute to society, education-based income might be an easier pill to swallow.

We have already pointed out the benefits that education provides. It enriches a culture, makes a country more competitive, reduces crime, and increases employment. Nice. But what if a country, local government, or even a neighborhood wants to offer paid education? What if they can't *afford* to do it? Well, it doesn't have to be as expensive as it sounds. The solution is to use a currency generated by the school itself. A school can create its own money! There is no need to tie this to state-generated currencies. In fact, there are many benefits to using your own currency.

First, you can create as much of it as you want. Say, for instance, a school offers to pay 100 of its own dollars for every unit of coursework that a student completes. Where does the money come from? The school *creates* it. All that is necessary to do this is a electronic ledger. It must be designed securely. Fortunately, best practices have already emerged from other electronic ledgers.

Great, you say, but that's just numbers on a ledger. What good is it for? It what sense is this "money"? It's not like you can walk into a store and buy a shirt or a loaf of bread with it.

Not yet. But you couldn't do much with Bitcoin at first, and now many retailers accept it. But before a new currency can gain wide use, it helps to create a consumer-exchange market. Think of this market like Ebay or Craigslist, but it only accepts the school's currency. I could list items I want to sell and other students can pay me using their currency from the school.

Or if the school chooses to, it can begin with its own store. Imagine Google opens a school. It will pay its students in Google currency. Google could then open a retail store (with a physical location, or just an online store) that accepts the currency. This would gives the money a perceived value. The products in the store give it value. And if students don't want what the store sells, they can trade the currency with other students who might want something from the store. Remember, a money's value comes from its ability to let people interact and exchange goods and services. The storefront would demonstrate to the students it is a viable currency. Then, with this in place, a market like Craigslist or Ebay could be set up. The students could use it to buy and sell things among themselves. When a marketplace grows large enough, the official school storefront can be eliminated altogether. The actual cost of "creating" this money would then be significantly lower than using state currency. The costs would be:

1. A secure and accurate account ledger.

2. A store with prizes that can be purchased with the school currency.

In theory, the success of the money would depend on its popularity and usage by the students. This would create a typical "Matthew Effect" – the more students a school can attract, the more widely used its currency will become. This puts the burden on the school to create the best program possible. But if a currency can gain enough strength, it might even be used to pay teachers and other staff salaries.

Further considerations:

Abuse of currency could be a problem. It's important to have transparent and secure accounting practices. I am not technically knowledgeable enough to know how to do this. But cryptocurrencies are already being used. Alternate currencies are found in video game systems. This money is used to buy things in the real world. It stands to reason that if we want to create a new currency that is safe and dependable, we can at least try.

Schools might unite with other schools to use a joint currency. This would expand the marketplace. It would be important to make the method of earning the currency as equivalent as possible in different schools. This might be difficult to gauge if based solely on achievement. But a time-based system might be one solution. One hundred hours logged in an environment should yield the same amount of money.

There are already online learning programs like Duolingo and Khan Academy that use coins or other reward points. For the most part, these points cannot be used as a medium of exchange between students. Furthermore, there is a possibility for cheating the system when the learning is entirely online. It might be wiser (for now) to focus on brick-and-mortar schools that allow time-based monitoring and the presence of real teachers. Also, the lack of human connection is an increasing problem in the world today. Every hour we spend on screens is time lost building real-world bonds. Some social skills are still present online, but there are significant disadvantages. People dive deeper into their own reality tunnels. A major function of schools is to act as centers for a community. Real communities are bumpier and more diverse than self-selected communities. Connecting to others through media and electronic devices will never be the same as in-person communication.

It has grown increasingly apparent that social media and other tech companies have enormous power. Facebook, Twitter, and Google have influence because they direct and control what people can see. They act as windows to the world. Because of this power, do these companies have a responsibility beyond reaping massive profits? Tech companies argue that they are just the messenger of news and other trending topics, but this a gross understatement of their influence. In an era where anyone can generate headlines with a few keystrokes, and the most lurid items get the most clicks, social media and search services must take some responsibility for the world we live in. This can include policing fake news articles, but I think they can do better than that.

A school would be one way to do this. Schools create a culture of growth and progress. It would also be valuable to these tech companies too. If they have a school with students, they have immediate access to a hiring pool. They would know where students excel, plus have the opinions of the school's instructors. In this way a school can transition students toward work that a company focuses on. The schools would want to make their programs as appealing and impressive as possible. More students means a better hiring pool. It would also strengthen the school's currency and prestige.

The important thing to remember is that money is flexible. We can play with it to serve our interests.

Hoarding money by fewer individuals and corporations hurts a society. So we can think about ways to avoid this. One solution is to have money *decrease* in value over time. This is much easier to do with digital currency than with paper, coins, or other physical goods. Digital currency can be given an expiration date from the day you receive it. If you didn't spend it within a year, for instance, it would be deducted from your account. But once you spent it, the recipient would have another year to spend it themselves. Alternatively, the money might lose 5% of its value for each month that it is held. There are all kinds of possibilities. After all, many things that were units of exchange before money (food, for example), had an expiration date.

But if your money loses value over time, how would you save for the future? If you can't save a huge stash of cash, how can you save for a house, retirement, or other large expenses? Valid points, but remember that these currencies will not be replacing larger currencies like the dollar anytime soon. They are merely an attempt to bring more value and interaction to your immediate community. Rather than sending your money to faceless corporations, it would be used at the local level.

But we should also look at the larger historical trend we find ourselves in. Because of automation and robotics, we may well be entering an age of abundance. The scarcity mindset of the past is no longer necessary. We already have enough food to feed everyone on the planet, *if* we can learn to allocate it correctly. Our wars and petty divisions, according to Steven Pinker in *The Better Angels of Our*

Nature, are slowly receding. Yes, we still have political despots, crime, injustice, environmental disasters, and more, but this is the most innovative time that humanity has ever witnessed. *Nobody* can predict exactly what the world will look like in ten years. If we do begin acknowledging that access to education and healthcare are basic human rights, then there will be less need to protect yourself inside a castle of your own making. Education-based currencies are an attempt to provide a safety net for everyone. Because anyone can enter these schools, not just young people – anyone willing to make the attempt, however limited their intelligence, would receive compensation. That is all that any society can ask: that people make the attempt. A healthy society's role is to provide as many opportunities as possible.

This is what the online landscape already looks like. If you want to learn something, *anything*, there is more free education online every day. It may be articles, videos, or software, but the information is out there. As usual, the physical world lags behind the digital. But things are slowly changing. Online schools may be the first to experiment with these methods of generating currency (based on learning). But I'm hoping that we can bring this to the real world, where it is most needed.

At this point in history, we rely on government for many things we need: The country's infrastructure, roads, social security, environmental and consumer protection, maintaining nuclear arsenals. These are things too large for any local organization to handle. We cannot expect schools and community organizations to handle these problems. However, the larger solution to our long-term problems is *education*. We will not find any solutions without continuous opportunities for education.

What can we expect from an educated population? That's the exciting thing – *we don't know*. It is largely unpredictable. Just as we don't know what an artist will be creating in the future, we don't know what an educated generation of people will bring to the world. But I would rather have educated people seeking problems to our dilemmas than privately-funded think tanks. In reality, a school *is* a think tank. The difference between schools and Washington think tanks is that one is fueled by public interest, and one is driven by the dollars of a select few.

The nation-state is experiencing turbulence. Many young people lack the nationalistic impulse that is necessary to maintain a country. They are more likely to view themselves as global citizens. Their identity is not defined by race or location. As such, we may be witnessing the rise of "virtual nation states." People identify with various cultures, language systems, histories, religions. They put their money in offshore accounts, acquire alternate citizenships for tax purposes, and spend half of their time in other countries. In what sense do they "belong" to a country? For the modern human, citizenship has taken on new meaning. People expect a government to *serve* them, like a corporate service, and if it doesn't, they are glad to take their "business" elsewhere. An alternative currency allows us to quickly and peacefully defund political leaders.

The loss of political machinery might appear frightening. But it doesn't have to be. In fact, there are many advantages to decentralizing our power structure. The internet itself was created to allow a decentralized network in the event of nuclear war. Yet we have not taken full advantage of it. A decentralized structure of cooperative cells may be our best protection against terrorism. Our identities don't need to be tied to a physical location, and decentralized collectives are more difficult to disrupt. We still link our power structures to national and state capitols, making them easy targets for terrorism. Compare this with something like Wikipedia. How would you go about "attacking" Wikipedia? True, you might hack their website or otherwise impede service, but it can be hosted on mirror sites and backed up. Removing any of the people behind it will not slow it down. Now imagine a "government" that looks more like Wikipedia than Washington DC. People could take part in the system of their choice, reaping the benefits from anywhere on Earth. To be a citizen would be a self-selection process, not based on location. Power structures don't need to be coercive, top-down tyrannies. They can be elective, bottom-up systems. The best governments (which is essentially what I'm proposing with the concept of school-based money) would be the most *effective*.

Returning to the presence of terrorism in the world today: The nation-state's response is to tighten borders, increase police and security, heighten surveillance, and do its best to keep terrorists from slipping through its net. This is highly impractical (if not impossible) due to the nature of terrorism.

Anyone with the right motivation can become a terrorist. It can be a disgruntled civil servant or a child stumbling onto the wrong website.

Terrorism is best understood through the context of *memes*. It may just be a helpful metaphor, but let's consider them. Richard Dawkins created the term *meme* to indicate a unit of cultural information transmitted from one mind to another. Tying your shoes is a meme. So is kissing someone, playing a video game, or wearing a tie. *Violence* is still a powerful meme in the world today. If your mind hasn't learned the tools to bypass violence, it is easy to see it as a way to get what you want. We are, according to the theory of natural selection, closely related to the great apes, and much human behavior is little better than the glorified actions of a domesticated primate. We often try to live by our higher selves, using intellect instead of instinct, but instinct is very powerful. Apes are raised tribally, and anyone not connected to the tribe is an enemy. While it would be nice if all of humanity saw itself as one vast tribe, this has never been the case. Learning to overcome Us vs. Them thinking is humanity's great challenge. Great thinkers from the Buddha, Jesus, Socrates, Mark Twain, Abraham Lincoln, Mother Theresa, Martin Luther King, Jr., and countless others have tried to help us overcome our innate aggression. But our biology is always with us. Testosterone is very powerful and cannot be overcome without awareness and intention.

It is tempting to blame the government and corporations for the world's problems. After all, they are huge and beyond the control of any single individual. It is easy to feel overwhelmed and insignificant in the face of such powerful forces. But remember: governments, corporations, and organizations are not things you can point to. They are more like software than hardware, and they primarily reside *in our heads*. And like software, they affect our behavior and how we interact. The great thing about software is that you can change it. And if enough people change the software they are using, it changes the whole world.

Many people join terrorist groups in desperation. They may live under a weak or corrupt governments, and groups like Boko Haram, Al-Qaeda, the Taliban, and Islamic State seem to offer an escape route. If you live in a war-torn country, it might appear that there is little difference between these groups and the official government. As such, you will probably choose the more powerful group. When there is no infrastructure, stability, or prospect for employment, terrorist groups provide the nearest equivalent. Trying to fight terrorism with guns and soldiers may actually strengthen these groups. It gives them something to resist. It makes the United States and its allies look like the oppressors. And few things bring people together better than a common enemy.

The U.S. Department of Defense struggles to fight terrorist groups. As the largest employer on Earth, the Department of Defense increasingly moves into non-war fields such as healthcare and education. This "mission creep" is inevitable. While the number of wars has decreased, the devastation a single war causes can be devastating. Yet the

Department of Defense is still firmly aligned in a war stance that directs its funding. If it hopes to remain relevant, it must begin the transition to peace. The best way to do this is with the memetic weapon of *education*. Good ideas and opportunities are more coercive than any soldier or weapon.

If we view terrorism as a memetic infection – a bleeding out of a bad idea – the solution is obvious. Rather than fighting it with armies and weapons, we should fight it *memetically*. I don't mean through propaganda (although this already takes place). Political spin is impossible to avoid anyway. But more powerful than spin and propaganda are genuine opportunities. This is what a school can provide. A school that pays you to attend creates an energy outlet more powerful than violence. A school can be an income, a chance to connect with others in a meaningful way, and an opportunity to learn and have fun. I'm not suggesting we set up schools in the most dangerous and contested warzones. But I am suggesting we create as many opportunities for education as possible. We can use local teachers, local resources. It doesn't help if the staff is made up entirely of foreigners. The funds may come from elsewhere, but the goal is the create a fountainhead *within* the community.

What can be taught at these schools? This really depends on the community and its needs. But *tools* with immediate benefits seems more important than *ideologies*. What are the relevant needs of the community? This could include practical applications like agriculture, house-building, and medicine, or more globally incentivized skills like programming, language skills, math, and engineering.

We don't need to limit these schools to other countries, however. Anyone in a modern city can see the problems of the current economic model. However much American politicians spout about equality, the U.S. is not a level playing field. We live in a caste system. Money is its basis. If you have more money, you have more rights, and more freedom. Money allows you to go places that the poor cannot. It frees you from a workplace that you dislike. It lets you develop your full potential. You even have rights to better healthcare and treatment. Let's put the euphemisms aside: Capitalism is a caste system.

As a boy, I seemed all too aware of this. I grew up in a lower-middle class suburb. I dreamed of being a burglar and stealing from the rich. I couldn't understand why a boy born into a different family could have access to so much more than me.

I read voraciously, thinking that education would offer a way out. I also didn't see why money should slow down my education. After all, couldn't Bill Gates' kids get any book they wanted? To counter this, I became an expert at shoplifting books. There was no guilt or shame involved. I was stealing from a faceless corporation, after all.

One day I was in a large bookstore and had my backpack with me. I proceeded to collect some items and take them to a quiet corner of the store where I knew no cameras or employees would see me. I looked the books over for security devices and removed them. Then I stuffed the books into my backpack. There was probably a hundred dollars worth of books in my bag, and this wasn't the first time I had been so bold. Casually making my way toward the exit, I slowed my breathing and walking speed so I would appear relaxed. All was going well. But as I walked through the retail security device, a blaring alarm sounded. No! I must have missed one of the RFID tags and set it off.

I didn't run, but I didn't stop. I acted like the alarm was for someone else, somewhere else. But certainly not *me*. I had places to be, and was out of the store.

Someone was following me. A tall guy wearing a tie, a clerk from the bookstore. Damn. "Hey, stop!" he said.

"What?" I said.

"You set off the alarm."

"That wasn't me."

"I *saw* you set it off," he said. "You were the only one going through the system."

I stayed calm. "Listen," I said. "I just bought a CD at the store across the street and it's in my bag. It probably has a security tag that set your system off."

I actually *had* just bought a compact disc (this was the 1990s, by the way). I took it out and showed him the CD and my receipt. He looked them over. He clearly didn't believe me. But he was probably not heavily invested in the job and didn't want trouble. He sighed, shook his head, and went back in the store.

It was a minor victory for me. Yes, I got away with some merchandise, but I had come too close to getting arrested for shoplifting. However much I might want to steal things, I decided that it wasn't the best path. But even if I stopped shoplifting, I still felt that education was something everyone has a right to.

The internet has dramatically changed the face of education. You can now learn tons of things free with apps, online courses, and videos. And not just education. People expect more and more online material to be free. Whether it's maps and driving directions, films, messaging services, or software, the competitive nature of the Web means that offering something for free gives you an edge over your competitors. Jeremy Rifkin describes this well in *The Zero Marginal Cost Society*. There seems to be no limit to what may become free in the digital world.

As this transition continues online, it creates a mindset in users. They *expect* things to be free. There might be bonus versions that you can pay for, premium subscriptions to go ad-free, but people expect basic versions to be free. We rarely think about the cost for searching online. We're not paying for that search, not with money. Google's advertisers are. We pay with our attention. As Douglas Rushkoff puts it, we are the product being sold to the advertisers, our eyeballs, and our minds.

Many websites struggle with this model. Traditional media outlets like newspapers create paywalls. If you want to read everything on a site like the New York Times, you need to pay a subscription fee. Only a small fraction of the audience bothers to bypass these annoying attempts to get our money. Other media websites try the traditional ad-based model and find that their revenue isn't enough to support their staff.

A possible solution: What if websites created their *own* currency? Imagine going to a website and reading an article. At the end of the article is a short quiz. You answer a few questions, and then receive one of the website's "dollars" in your online account. This quiz, like a CAPTCHA, and an account linked to your Facebook profile, for instance, can keep people from scamming the system. Obviously you want to avoid fraud with any currency, and new methods will be created to ensure that. But any popular website can create its own economy through the attention of its users. People can and should be incentivized (not penalized with a paywall) to regularly come to your website. The more popular the site is, the larger currency it can generate. And as with a school-based currency, a marketplace for goods can be created that will ultimately be self-sustaining. Websites can form alliances for shared currencies and so on.

There are already experiments with this – sites like Steemit allow users to post links, with more popular links earning users more of the site's cryptocurrency. This currency can be exchanged for Bitcoin. But there is no reason that a site has to create a new format to have its own currency. The potential is already out there. Any site that people want to look at is a potential source for new currency. This reminds me of one of my favorite Marshall McLuhan quotes: "It's misleading to suppose there's any basic difference between education and entertainment. This distinction merely relieves people of the responsibility of looking into the matter."

Aside from corporations and websites, traditional schools are also well-situated to create their own money. Countries like Brazil, Norway, Germany, Finland, Slovenia, Sweden, and France offer free or low cost tuition. Even in the United States, community colleges in Tennessee and San Francisco are experimenting with free tuition programs. Why not take these programs a step further and *pay* students in a cryptocurrency? The currency can be linked to getting a passing grade. Once again, it doesn't have to cost a lot to get it started. Allow the currency to be used in the student store, and set up a marketplace to let students interact with each other using the money.

To summarize, the general process for creating these currencies is this:

1. Set up an online accounting system. This can include a blockchain, and apps for sending and receiving the currency. A phone can be used to pay with the currency online or in-person.

2. Create a clear, consistent, and transparent method for earning and generating the currency. This method should prevent abuse, theft, and not allow scammers, employees of the organization/corporation itself, or bots to obtain currency illegitimately. This may require a blockchain, AI surveillance, CAPTCHA-like tests or quizzes, or accountants, depending on the sophistication and scale of the system. An organization might incentivize its employees with a salary in the currency, but this salary should be transparent.

3. If the currency has a deflation or expiration rate, it should be clear to its users.

4. Once students/consumers start receiving the currency, a store should be created to let them use their funds. This store can be online or brick-and-mortar. It doesn't need to be fancy. The "store" can even be a person who keeps track of and dispenses items when the students are ready to redeem their currency. Again, this depends on the size of the organization and number of people using the currency. If the school feels there is already enough "confidence" in the currency, the storefront may be skipped.

5. A marketplace can now be created to let the students interact with each other using the currency (like Ebay or Craigslist). The marketplace can be entirely online and self-regulated by the students, or it can be a regular event like a swap meet. If it is an event, it may be combined with the storefront of step 4.

6. Adjustments may be made in the method of dispensing currency and the deflation rate to maintain a robust currency.

7. A currency may be linked with other schools or traded with other currencies on an exchange.

8. As a currency grows, local businesses may be solicited to accept the currency.

9. Given enough usage, larger businesses and websites can be solicited to accept the currency.

This method is applicable at the local level (your church, for example). And it is also scalable to the largest corporations (if Google or Apple open a school, for instance). Employers can pay bonuses in their own currency to employees – they already do this in the form of stock payments. A currency provides more flexibility, however, since the amount is not connected to a company's funds.

The key point is that money is flexible and virtually anyone is in a position to create a currency. The current economic model maintains the class hierarchy found throughout history, albeit under a different name. At present, having more money guarantees you more rights and more freedom.

More and more lower and middle class individuals recognize this. Populist movements and slimy politicians seize on this unrest. They say they will restore wealth ("jobs") to the disenfranchised. But this is just the old model under a different name. Rather than create opportunities for all, populist movements aim to restore power to *my group*. Never mind the rights of foreigners – they aren't quite the same as me. As long as I get mine, things will be fine.

Populist leaders focus on extremism. They do this by preying on the fear and ignorance of their constituents. Someone can always be blamed. Hatred can always be stirred. This is tapping into the most basic "Us vs. Them" mentality that we have as primates. This *fundamentalism* is not limited to any group of people or belief system. It is not confined to any ethnicity, religion, gender, or age group. It is a frame of mind that can take hold anywhere.

Education is what allows people to move

beyond fundamentalism. It is why education is so essential to our societal development. True learning is a mindset that requires continual adaptation and progress. It is completely at odds with fundamentalism. This requires no magical thinking to understand. New tools and literacies create fresh perspectives for a growth mindset. A person trained in a new technology or art sees possibilities that an unskilled person cannot.

New forms of money can be the fulcrum that pushes us toward a new society. Just as capitalism pushed us into the Industrial Revolution, education-based and attentional currencies can push us into a Learning Revolution. In its current form, money is infected with authoritarianism, conformity, oppression, and violence. Trying to reform old money is an uphill battle. Far easier to create a new form of money and give it a bias toward compassion, peace, humor, and creativity.

Just as slavery and serfdom were acceptable for centuries, it will take time for people to wake up to the inherent injustice of the current economic model. Nation-states and the wealthy are well aware of it, and they hold tight to the power they have. They pander to the least educated and keep the energy flowing toward marketing and consumption. This has maintained their power structures until now. But we have seen web services rise and fall overnight. All the money in every bank can be made worthless at any time, and this frightens them. It need not frighten you. The idea that things will get "out of control" begs the question: Out of *whose* control?

When I speak to Lyft and Uber drivers, I find

employees with no great affection for their employer. Many of them have stickers on their windows for *both* companies. They are not technically regarded as employees, but contractors, to be tossed aside when the company gets driverless cars. This seems to be the impetus of the current economy. This is not community interaction – it is capitalism and its grinding gears. People send their money thousands of miles away and the community suffers. This is what happens when money becomes our default method of interaction. Social skills and manners collapse, and everyone is viewed as a service. The only option seems to be to keep running on the hamster wheel, buy more goodies, and build a higher fence to keep the "bad" people out. The distance between neighbors increases. Instead, people find alignment and connection through online communities of avatars.

But we can rewrite this *now*. We may not be "ready," but we will not arrive by being ready. We will get there by *going* there. New economic systems will obviously face new challenges of their own. But witness the cost of the current model: poor healthcare, oppressive jobs, crippling debt, environmental destruction, and pointless wars. We owe it to ourselves to try something better.

RECOMMENDED READING

Here are some books I recommend to learn more about these ideas.

War No More (Library of America anthology), edited by Lawrence Rosenwald

Throwing Rocks at the Google Bus by Douglas Rushkoff

The One World Schoolhouse by Salman Khan

The Attention Merchants by Tim Wu

The Zero Marginal Cost Society by Jeremy Rifkin

Sapiens and *Homo Deus* by Yuval Noah Harari

The Art of Asking by Amanda Palmer

Wonderland by Steven Johnson

The Medium is the Massage by Marshall McLuhan

The Better Angels of Our Nature by Steven Pinker

Inevitable by Kevin Kelly

The Meme Machine by Susan Blackmore

Reality is Broken by Jane McGonigal

Darwin's Unfinished Symphony by Kevin N. Laland

How Everything Became War and the Military Became Everything by Rosa Brooks

ALSO BY ADAM SAVAGE

Overcoming Writer's Block: How to Unleash Your Creativity and Inner Genius When Writing

Tarot for Beginners: The Complete Guide to Tarot Cards

www.ingramcontent.com/pod-product-compliance
Lightning Source LLC
Chambersburg PA
CBHW050035230526
45470CB00003B/1282